MEMORIAL TO THE FUTURE

VOLKER von TÖRNE
MEMORIAL TO THE FUTURE

Translated by Jean Boase-Beier
with Anthony Vivis

Guest edited by
Philip Wilson

Introduction by
David Wheatley

2017

Published by Arc Publications,
Nanholme Mill, Shaw Wood Road
Todmorden OL14 6DA, UK
www.arcpublications.co.uk
Original poems copyright © 1981, Verlag Klaus Wagenbach, Berlin
Translation copyright © Jean Boase-Beier 2017
Introduction copyright © David Wheatley 2017
Copyright in the present edition © Arc Publications 2017

978 1910345 64 1 (pbk)
978 1910345 65 8 (hbk)
978 1910345 66 5 (ebk)

Acknowledgements

The publishers are grateful to Verlag Klaus Wagenbach for permission to reproduce poems from *Im LandeVogelfrei* by Volker von Törne both in the original German and in English translation.

Design by Tony Ward
Printed in Great Britain by T.J. International Ltd,
Padstow, Cornwall

Cover picture: Tony Ward

This book is in copyright. Subject to statutory exception and to provision of relevant collective licensing agreements, no reproduction of any part of this book may take place without the written permission of Arc Publications.

The translation of these poems was supported by a grant from the Goethe Institut which is funded by the German Ministry of Foreign Affairs.

Arc Publications 'Visible Poets' series
Series Editor: Jean Boase-Beier

CONTENTS

Series Editor's Note / 7
Translator's Preface / 9
Introduction / 13

20 / Wassili am Weg	• Vasily on the Road / 21
22 / Endlösung	• Final Solution / 23
24 / Deutscher Psalm	• German Psalm / 25
26 / Abschied	• Leaving / 27
28 / Wege	• Paths / 29
30 / Rauch	• Smoke / 31
32 / Was mir die Leute sagen	• What People Tell Me / 33
34 / Erinnerung an die Zukunft	• Memorial to the Future / 35
44 / An Hölty	• To Hölty / 45
46 / Pogrom	• Pogrom / 47
50 / Erinnerung an einen Oberlehrer	• Memorial to a Schoolmaster / 51
52 / Krähenflügel	• The Wing of the Crow / 53
54 / Am Wegrand	• By the Wayside / 55
56 / Wege der Asche	• On Paths of Ashes / 57
60 / Herbstfeier	• Autumn Festival / 61
62 / Sieger der Geschichte	• History's True Heroes / 63
66 / Elegie (1)	• Elegy (1) / 67
68 / Nachricht	• Message / 69
70 / Arbeitgeber	• Employer / 71
72 / An Attila József	• To Attila József / 73
74 / Masurischer Sommer	• Summer in the Masurian Lakes / 75
76 / Mittagslicht	• Midday Light / 77
78 / Elegie (2)	• Elegy (2) / 79
80 / Am Schreibtisch	• At this Desk / 81
84 / Diesseits	• Over Here / 85
86/ Im Fahrtwind	• In the Rush of Air / 87
88 / Nachmittagsbesuch	• An Afternoon Visit / 89
90 / Vaterlandslos	• Free of my Fatherland / 91

92 / Epigramm	Epigram / 93
94 / Frühlingsgedicht	Spring Song / 95
96 / Flugblatt	Flyer / 97
98 / Selbstgespräch	Soliloquy / 99
100 / Rückzug	Withdrawal / 101
102 / Notstand	State of Emergency / 103
104 / Anrufung meines Engels	I Call upon my Angel / 105
106 / Beim Lesen der Zeitung	While Reading the Paper / 107
108 / Stunde der Wölfe	Hour of the Wolves / 109
110 / Gedanken im Mai	Thoughts in May / 111
112 / Bilder	Images / 113
114 / An Ahasver	To Ahasuerus / 115
116 / An Hölderlin	To Hölderlin / 117
118 / Notstandsübung	Emergency Drill / 119
120 / Eiszeit	Ice Age / 121
122 / Erinnerung an Carl Sandburg	Remembering Carl Sandburg / 123
124 / Auf dem Boden des Grundgesetzes (1976)	The Constitution, 1976 / 125
126 / Kriegsspiel	War Game / 127
128 / Regierungserklärung	A Statement by the Government / 129
130 / Pastorale	Pastoral / 131
134 / Trinkspruch	Drinking Song / 135
136 / Liebesgedicht	Love Poem / 137
138 / Zu Beginn der Achtzigerjahre. Nach Catull	At the Start of the Eighties. After Catullus / 139

Biographical Notes / 140

SERIES EDITOR'S NOTE

The 'Visible Poets' series was established in 2000, and set out to challenge the view that translated poetry could or should be read without regard to the process of translation it had undergone. Since then, things have moved on. Today there is more translated poetry available and more debate on its nature, its status, and its relation to its original. We know that translated poetry is neither English poetry that has mysteriously arisen from a hidden foreign source, nor is it foreign poetry that has silently rewritten itself in English. We are more aware that translation lies at the heart of all our cultural exchange; without it, we must remain artistically and intellectually insular.

One of the aims of the series was, and still is, to enrich our poetry with the very best work that has appeared elsewhere in the world. And the poetry-reading public is now more aware than it was at the start of this century that translation cannot simply be done by anyone with two languages. The translation of poetry is a creative act, and translated poetry stands or falls on the strength of the poet-translator's art. For this reason 'Visible Poets' publishes only the work of the best translators, and gives each of them space, in a Preface, to talk about the trials and pleasures of their work.

From the start, 'Visible Poets' books have been bilingual. Many readers will not speak the languages of the original poetry but they, too, are invited to compare the look and shape of the English poems with the originals. Those who can are encouraged to read both. Translation and original are presented side-by-side because translations do not displace the originals; they shed new light on them and are in turn themselves illuminated by the presence of their source poems. By drawing the readers' attention to the act of translation itself, it is the aim of these books to make the work of both the original poets and their translators more visible.

Jean Boase-Beier

TRANSLATOR'S PREFACE

I first came across Volker von Törne's poetry in the 1980s, when I lived in Germany. It was read in schools and by university students, but, in spite of being well-known enough to be included in Karl Otto Conrady's vast 1977 anthology *Das große deutsche Gedichtbuch* (The Big Book of German Poetry) alongside the work of poets like Sarah Kirsch and Wolf Biermann, his work never achieved the fame of that of many of his contemporaries. Apart from one or two poems, his work has not been translated into English.

What first struck me about von Törne's poems, and made me want to translate them, was their intensity, which was combined with the ironic distancing and the feeling almost of lightness that came from his use of common German idioms and colloquialisms.

The intensity comes from the weight of guilt and anger in so many of the poems. He felt personally guilty that his father had been in the SS and that he had, as a small child in the late 1930s, repeated the phrases he heard about German Nationalism, about the need for racial purity and the desire to conquer others. But he was also very aware of the collective guilt of the German people, and angry at the attempt of so many to try simply to forget or even to insist they had known nothing. Alongside the guilt and anger is often a strong sense of longing and nostalgia – longing for a world in which people would be able to face the evils of the past and offer atonement, and nostalgia for a time when he did not know what he knows now, at the time of writing. The sense of an idyllic world tainted, in one's memory of it, with the knowledge of what then was still to come, is very strong in poems like 'Summer in the Masurian Lakes' (p. 75). For the translator, this depth of feeling, this weight of memory, needs to be carried over into English. Often it is a small, precise image – the approaching shadows, in the poem above, the headless hens in 'Pastoral' (p. 131) – that turns the idyll into a place that seems to be waiting for everything to change. But images are not difficult to convey: we can all imagine woods, fields, paths, lakes, the sound of saws cutting the trees down, the sight of encroaching shade. It is the language, so firmly rooted in the idiomatic German of the 1960s and 1970s, a time of great political and social upheaval, that can prove difficult.

Von Törne makes many allusions in his poems to the poets he read as a child, such as Friedrich Hölderlin, a particular favourite, and also to Bertolt Brecht. Some of his poems are consciously written in imitation of Brecht: 'Thoughts in May' (p. 111), in which he describes how he must live with the guilt not only of Germany's past but also of present inequalities, takes its overall theme, and even individual phrases, from Brecht's famous poem 'To Those Born Later'. He shares Brecht's concern with 'rough thinking' (sometimes rendered as 'crude thinking'), for which Brecht's phrase was 'das plumpe Denken' – thinking which is unadorned and not refined by philosophy or layers of meta-thinking but just *is*, as we find it in everyday idioms. It is this thinking that needs to be fully understood and examined.

Like Brecht, von Törne believed in the importance of critical and poetic distance: his idioms and colloquialisms are turned round, placed in a different context, and so appear in a new light. Children play war-games but war-games are also the games war plays with us ('War Game', p. 127). Germans, we are told, are good at clearing up. Clearing up *what*, we wonder ('Epigram', p. 93).

There are many echoes of Brecht, but von Törne's voice is very different. The weight of grief, guilt and melancholy overlays even the most delicately personal poems, such as 'Love Poem' (p. 137), where he cannot help but see the drawing of the curtains not just as a simple act of ensuring privacy but also as a way of shutting out, for a time, the branches 'heavy with stars'. 'Stars' is one of the words, like 'ashes', 'smoke', 'night', that occur regularly in the poems, and signal the constant presence of the Holocaust in the poet's psyche. For the translator, such words must be sacrosanct: to lose them would be to lose the context for everything the poems say.

But the main difficulty for the translator is neither the images nor the words, but the careful balance between hope and pain, longing and despair, which must be preserved in order to ensure that von Törne's voice – despairing, angry, yet also ironic, funny, and flippant (as in his 'Drinking Song' about Hitler, p. 135) – comes through in English.

In order to try and do this, I have spent many years reading von Törne's poems, but also finding out what I can about his life, about what his friends have said, above all about the *Aktion Sühnezeichen Friedensdienste* (Action Reconciliation-Service for Peace), the Christian left-wing organisation that was founded in 1958 with an admission of German guilt for the war and the Holocaust and a pledge to make reparation. It has gone on to promote peace and understanding through actions to help victims of oppression throughout the world. Von Törne was one of its Director from 1963 until his early death in 1980, and one of his plans, only to come to fruition after his death, was the International Youth Meeting Centre in Auschwitz.

For there is another aspect of von Törne's voice that the translator needs to hear, but which is only, perhaps, really clear in the context of his life, his letters and his interactions with friends: he was a man who was full of energy, who was driven – in the end beyond endurance – by the need to do something rather than just think about it. He was filled with the nervous restlessness of the chronically ill and a mixture of despair, resignation, and the sense of how much remains to be done; these feelings are particularly evident in his 'Catullus' poem (p. 139), written in the year of his death.

The facts of his life suggest a character full of drive and impatience, sympathetic, warm-hearted, and often angry and argumentative. We can hear these characteristics in the very many short lines, questions, exhortations to get on and do something, that fill his poems. It seems especially important, then, in translating the poems, to pay careful attention to layout, and to the length of lines and the structure of sentences.

I began the translation of these poems fifteen years ago, working in collaboration with my friend Anthony Vivis, the translator of German drama. We had very different ways of working. I tend to concentrate on words and structures and images: What do wolves suggest? Why a crow? Why does he leave out an auxiliary in 'While Reading the Paper' (p. 107)? Anthony, on the other hand, would focus on the physical voice in the poems, the colloquialisms, the feeling for what we would say in English. It would be hard to imagine more different ways of doing it. Yet the collaboration (on this and other projects) was exhilarating *because* of these differences.

When Anthony died in 2013, our translations were still unfinished. As I took them up again to add to them, to rework them, to rethink them, I found not only many handwritten notes from Anthony about this legendary animal or that poem by Hölderlin, but also the inevitable coffee stains, torn scraps of paper, and the faint scent of damp carpets, which helped me to recall many of our conversations about individual poems. I have revised extensively, but have tried, where I could, not to impose my interpretation and my voice as translator at the expense of Anthony's. If this leaves the English poems more ambiguous, so much the better. They are poems that demand to be reread many times.

Jean Boase-Beier

INTRODUCTION

Irish poet James Clarence Mangan was among the most prolific conduits between German and English poetry in the nineteenth century, but was not without eccentricities in his approach to 'the task of the translator.' Struggling with the paradox, for a Romantic translator, that the spirit of the people is unreproducibly present in the original language, he abandons the idea of literalist fidelity in translation. Instead, the translator must "always improve on his original if he can", leaving the original "essentially unrecognisable in English". Hailing Charles Anster's 1835 translation of the first part of *Faust*, he promotes Anster over Goethe's head: "he has translated that part of the mind of Goethe which was unknown to Goethe himself [...] he is, in short, the real author of *Faust*". Rather than being welcomed into English by his translator, Goethe is evicted from his own text by Anster. Another homeless wanderer, and one who provides a point of connection between Mangan and Volker von Törne, is Ahasuerus, the Wandering Jew of myth. Like Ahasuerus, the narrator of Mangan's 'An Extraordinary Adventure in the Shades' seeks refuge "now in a cavern and now in a pothouse", while von Törne's Ahasuerus sings to awaken "the ashes of the dead / stitching them shoes / for their journey back." It is a fitting metaphor for the afterlife of this German poet, too little known in English, but von Törne has weightier matters in mind than his literary posterity. To encounter a poem titled 'Endlösung' ('Final Solution') at the beginning of this collection is to confront the dark heart of von Törne's art. Did Paul Celan ever permit himself such a direct naming of his unspeakable theme? Yet, no less audaciously, the poem itself is a mere fourteen words long. Loquacity and silence play out a surprisingly two-sided dialogue. This is a poet raised by "murderers", we read, "who brought me up as their own / In their image", and who "called that slaughterhouse / My Fatherland." Disarming frankness is only half the story, as von Törne struggles with an answering impulse to "close my eyes / pull out the fuse / smash the screen", and refuse all communication. "When the great terror came, / I fell dumb", von Törne's older contemporary Nelly Sachs wrote of confronting the same challenge, from her German-Jewish perspective. There are many ways beyond the literal for silence to find its mysteriously translated voice.

Amtliche Mitteilung, von Törne's début, appeared in 1961, the same year as Johannes Bobrowski's, entering a landscape in which Paul Celan (b. 1920) was already well established and Hans Magnus Enzensberger (b. 1929; début collection, 1957) would soon confirm his pre-eminence with a Büchner Prize (1963). With his patchy experience of translation, however, von Törne remains for his Anglophone readers very much a man on the fringes, waiting to come in from the cold. "Not every ending is also a beginning / Colossal bridges carry streets that lead nowhere", he writes in 'German Psalm', a poem politely turning from metaphors of reconstruction. "The end is in the beginning and yet you go on", Beckett proposed in his own anti-reconstructive response to the war, *Endgame*. Placed third here, 'German Psalm' gets more than a little ahead of itself, in its valedictory tone and embrace of the dead-end. Beckett, again, was well versed in the openings presented by the brick wall: "No future in this. Alas yes" (*Worstward Ho*). Still, it is far from easy going. The poet von Törne may most forcefully remind Anglophone readers of is Tadeusz Różewicz, laureate of '60s anti-poetry, whose skeletally reduced lines he shares, and seeming auto-allergic reaction to the very existence of his poetry after the great catastrophe. How tentatively, as though against its own better instincts, 'Leaving' makes its way down the page:

> The sweetness of summer
> Has melted
> On our tongues
>
> The leaves
> Flood
> Over the paths

>   The swallows scrawl
>   Leaving
>   In the air

In British poetry of the '60s, the Movement and its "confident Lowbrowism" (Charles Tomlinson) showed strong resistance to rupturings of the lyric line of the kind practised by contemporary German poetry. Only with the launch of *Modern Poetry in Translation* and the *Penguin Modern European Poets* list did the more dissonant music of European verse have a chance to untune the ingrained habits of the Anglophone ear. Tomlinson proselytised in Britain for the Objectivist poets, and Charles Reznikoff or Carl Rakozi would have found much to enjoy in von Törne's stripped-down yet bountiful landscapes.

The question of naming and reference remains an obstinate dilemma. Michael Hamburger, that keen observer of the post-war European scene, has written incisively of realism and anti-realist currents in post-war poetry: where a Ted Hughes poem about an animal might work its way up to an abstraction, a French one, with its aversion to the "agonizing tautology of the common word", might begin and remain on that level. Von Törne's case is somewhat different again. Consider the invitation to the reader of 'Paths': "Come with me. The drowned years / Are rising to the surface. Tonight / By the river the fires / Are burning again." What ways, what years, what fires?, we might ask; but the studied vagueness suggests, to borrow a line from Geoffrey Hill, that "this is more than enough", and that further questions may turn up some disturbing answers. With their lowering crows and wayside farmers, von Törne's poems pursue that Germanic variant on the *via dolorosa*, the *Winterreise*. These are recognisably landscapes of nineteenth-century Romanticism, but as surely as in Michael Haneke's *The White Ribbon*, something is up. Protestations of rootedness are shot through with desperation, as in 'Summer in the Masurian Lakes' ("Here / I want to stay / Sheltered / By wood.") Faust himself knew that asking the passing moment to linger was hopeless.

Alternating between obliquity and fractured confrontations with the unspeakable is not the only option taken up by von Törne. Brecht's example enables excursions into longer narrative verse; 'Thoughts in May' is a remarkable first cousin to the Berliner's 'Of Poor B. B.':

> I speak of myself: Volker von Törne, born
> In the thirty-fourth year of the twentieth century
> While my comrades were fighting the murderers
> Who brought me up as their own
>   In their image:
> And I drank the milk
> Denied to the starving.

This is not, or not quite the "black milk of morning" drunk in Celan's *Todesfuge*, but von Törne knows how to make that milk curdle on the tongue. In 'What People Tell Me', the poet encounters the Adenauerian *Wirtschaftswunder* in the person of proud new fridge-owners, formalizing the *pax Germanica* with their consumer durables ("They think quite simply / of everything"). Rootedness becomes reconciliation with trashy transience ("I have set up house / Put down roots / In the private rented sector / Among supermarkets massage-parlours", 'Over Here'). Gottfried Benn in old age, that 'Man on the Dump' of post-war German poetry, would surely approve. Consumerism is merely the obverse of the Democratic Republic's paralysed dystopia, whose deep-frozen state he renders in 'Memorial to the Future', petrifying the political poem into mock-grandiose gestures ("The sky turns to stone / above the city"). The poem ventriloquizes a public voice in a state where no such voice can meaningfully exist. Here as elsewhere (cf. 'Pogrom') when von Törne resorts to the poetry of direct statement, the pathos can sound painfully exposed ("Truth is simple like water / and bread"). Solidarity is the solidarity of the utterly routed, of "ashes / in the wind, like all my brothers / forgotten". There is an infinite amount of hope, as Kafka darkly wise-cracked, but not for us.

The '60s and '70s were a fertile time for protest poetry, with Adrian Mitchell's 'Tell Me Lies About Vietnam' and the Penguin anthology *Poems of the Committed Individual* in English, and not a few of von Törne's poems would lend themselves to speeches from the podium at PEN conferences or addresses to the crowd at a CND rally. But here too there is ambivalence. Von Törne breaks away from Paul Celan's elliptical style but cannot commit his poems to full-time *engagé* status. The political remains a zone of danger and wounding, subject to furtive poetic raids, but not somewhere the poem is best advised to put down its troubled roots. Contemplating its all-powerful dictator figure, 'Memorial to the Future' announces that "He is more mighty than God". One visionary figure who has struck many modern German poets as "more mighty than God" is the great Swabian Romantic addressed in 'To Hölderlin', a voice of luminous grace even as his mind clouded:

> *Make matchwood*
> *of your dragon-ship, o Bellarmin!*
>
> Laden with the feathers of the Fundevogel
> with fragments of the glass mountain
> horns of plenty
> and divining rods
> you go on your way
> tapping the heavens
> in search of the buried sea.

Bellarmin, a reference to the character in Hölderlin's novel *Hyperion*, might also make the reader think of the Jesuit Roberto Bellarmino, Galileo's accuser, while Fundevogel is the Foundling-Bird, the Protean transformer of the Grimm Brothers' fairy tale. Galilean parallels return in 'The Constitution', whose parroting of "basic principles / of freedom and democracy" comes with a heavy admixture of sarcasm. "Only heretics" make trouble by questioning "Whether / The sun really revolves / Around the earth."

In their cautious way, von Törne's poems perform repeated acts of approach and withdrawal from the public sphere and the robust styles of engagement honed in the '60s by Enzensberger and Grass. When he describes a violent police response to a demonstration in 'Emergency Drill', we feel the pressure raining down on the poem too to stand its ground or duck for cover. When he conjures visions of a climate deep-freeze in 'Ice Age', the prospect seems more than a little grimly attractive. Paul Celan too had his visions of a new ice age in 'Eis, Eden', and (in Geoffrey Hill's translation) of "split selfhoods, conjugat[ing] / ice-facets from the air". Returning to von Törne's landscape writing, in 'Pastoral', we sense again his preference for bracing Northern tableaux, so reminiscent of Bobrowski. Even within the short-lined stanzas of 'Pastoral', he practises a form of rhopalic contraction down to the single agonized detail on which so much depends:

4

Through the forests saws
Sing, in the farmyard
Hens flutter
Headless

5

I know nothing of the beginning
I know nothing of the end
What I move is what
Moves me

His poetic map is most intimately bound up with the "slaughter-house" of the "Fatherland", but von Törne's is an *oeuvre* with widely-branching roots, as witness his translation from Catullus and salute to a tragic Hungarian precursor, 'To Attila József'. Against the voices counselling the Hungarian to *"Go over there"*, von Törne urges him to "Stay with us, brother". Caught between inducements to flee the unspeakable and the need to tarry and bear witness, von Törne's is a poetry of powerfully conflicting imperatives. It is also, however, a poetry alive to the enduring surprise "Of the sweet-smelling limes", even if we must follow it "Under the gallows-branches" to enjoy to the full its heady and feverish pleasures.

David Wheatley

MEMORIAL TO THE FUTURE

WASSILI AM WEG

Wassili, zahnlos
Am Weg
      Damals die Deutschen
Seinen Sohn stellten sie hier
An die Wand
      Das Weiß
Der Mauer schmerzt
In den Augen

VASILY ON THE ROAD

Vasily, toothless
On the road
        Here on that day
The Germans stood his son
Against the wall
            The white
Of the wall
Pierces my eyes

ENDLÖSUNG

1

Die Juden
Sind unser
Unglück

2

Das haben
Wir immer
Gesagt

3

Das hat
Keiner
Gewußt

FINAL SOLUTION

   1

The Jews
Are our
Misfortune

   2

That's what
We've always
Said

   3

Only
None of us
Knew

DEUTSCHER PSALM

1

Die Hoffnung hat ihr Soll nicht erfüllt
Einzementiert wird der Zorn in den Kehlen

2

Brot sättigt nicht mehr und Wasser macht durstig
Mit Spruchbändern und Fahnen wird der Himmel verhängt

3

Erfüllt sind die Städte vom Schweigen der Steine
Wer erinnert sich noch unserer Träume?

4

Nicht jedes Ende ist auch ein Anfang
Über mächtige Brücken führen die Straßen ins Leere

GERMAN PSALM

1

Hope has not achieved its aim
Anger is cemented into people's throats

2

Bread no longer satisfies, water causes thirst
The sky is draped with flags and banners

3

Cities filled with the silence of stones
Can anyone still recall our dreams?

4

Not every ending is also a beginning
Colossal bridges carry streets that lead nowhere

ABSCHIED

Die Süße des Sommers
Zerging
Auf unsern Zungen

Über die Wege
Flutet
Das Laub

Abschied
Schreiben die Schwalben
Ins Blaue

LEAVING

The sweetness of summer
Has melted
On our tongues

The leaves
Flood
Over the paths

The swallows scrawl
Leaving
In the air

WEGE

1

Komm. Die versunkenen Jahre
Steigen herauf. Am Abend
Brennen wieder
Die Feuer am Fluß

2

Im Mondlicht glänzen die Tschakos
Der Gendarmen. Die Bauern
Lassen die Hunde los
Und verriegeln
Die Türen

3

Wir liegen am Fluß und lauschen
Dem Lied des Zigeuners. Der singt:
Meine Geige hat zwei Gefährten
Liebe heißen sie
Und Tod

4

Komm. Die Pferde scharren
Schon mit den Hufen. Offen
Liegen vor uns
Die Wege
Ins Land

PATHS

   1

Come with me. The drowned years
Are rising to the surface. Tonight
By the river the fires
Are burning again

   2

The gendarmes wear shakos
That glint in the moonlight. The farmers
Unleash their dogs
And bolt
Their doors

   3

We lie by the river, listening
To the gipsy's song. He sings:
My violin has two comrades
Their names are love
And death

   4

Come with me. The horses are scraping
The ground. Ahead of us
The paths
To the country
Lie clear

RAUCH

Für Reuwen

Einst lebte das Land. Grüne Wagen
Zogen durchs Dorf. Im Frühlicht
Schnaubten die Pferde
Am Fluß

Wohin sind sie gezogen, die Kesselflicker
Und Musikanten? An welchem Ufer
Weiden ihre Pferde? Unter welchem Mond singen ihre
Geigen?

Niemand hat sie gesehn. Spurlos
Rauch in den Wolken
Zogen sie
Fort

SMOKE
For Reuwen

This land was alive once. Green carts
Made their way through the village. In the first light
Horses snorted
By the river

Which way have the music-makers gone
And the tinkers? On what bank
Are their horses grazing now? Beneath what moon
Their violins singing?

No-one has seen them. Without a trace
Smoke in the clouds
They have gone
Away

WAS MIR DIE LEUTE SAGEN

Kauf dir einen Kühlschrank,
sagen sie mir, damit dir der Schnaps
im Sommer nicht warm wird. Lagere Koks ein,
sagen sie mir, der nächste Winter
kommt bestimmt.

Sie denken einfach
an alles.

WHAT PEOPLE TELL ME

Get yourself a fridge
they tell me, to make sure your schnapps
stays cool in the summer. Stock up on coke,
they tell me, another winter
is bound to come.

They think quite simply
of everything.

ERINNERUNG AN DIE ZUKUNFT

> *scandit aeratas vitiosa navis*
> *cura nec turmas equitum relinquit,*
> *ocior cervis et agente nimbos*
> *ocior Euro*
> HORAZ

1

Er hat die Durstenden in die Wüsten
geschickt. Die Frierenden hat er
dem Frost preisgegeben. Die Bettler
beutet er aus.

Seine Agenten sind überall. Vor dem Donner
seiner Maschinen erbeben
die Kontinente. Die Himmel
hallen wider
von seinem Ruhm.

(So wurde berichtet)

2

Auf alle Länder
hat er seinen Fuß gesetzt. Er
ist der Herr der Meere. Die Himmel
hat er mit Feuer erfüllt.

MEMORIAL TO THE FUTURE

> *scandit aeratas vitiosa navis*
> *cura nec turmas equitum relinquit,*
> *ocior cervis et agente nimbos*
> *ocior Euro*
> HORACE

1

He has sent the thirsty into the wilderness
and left the cold at the mercy
of the ice. He has stolen
from beggars.

His henchmen are all about. Continents
shudder at the thunder
of his planes. And the heavens
echo
with his glory.

(Or so we were told)

2

He has set his foot
into every land. He is
lord of the seas. He has filled
the heavens with his fire.

The epigraph is from Horace's *Odes,* Book II, no. 16, a poem about the longing for peace. Philip Wilson translates it thus:

Cruel care boards even armoured galleys,
never fails to harass the cavalry,
swifter than stags, and swifter than Eurus
    driving on clouds

Er ist mächtig wie Gott. Das Wasser der Flüsse
ist sein Eigentum und das schwarze Gestein
der Gebirge. Ihm gehört
das Fleisch auf den Weiden und der Fisch
in den Netzen. Er macht den Preis
für die Frucht auf den Feldern. Zu seinem Lob
treiben die Wälder
den Papiermühlen zu.

Er ist mächtiger als Gott. Für ihn
waschen die Bettler Gold aus den Flüssen. Für ihn
schlagen die Frierenden Glut aus den Schächten. Die Heimatlosen
bestellen seine Äcker. Die Hungernden tragen das Korn
in seine Speicher. Ihm zu Ehren
bauen die Obdachlosen
Städte aus Stein. Herr ist er
über Handlanger
und Tellerwäscher.

Herr ist er über die Angst. Die Klagenden
hat er geknebelt. Die Zornigen
hat er erschlagen. Die Sintflut
ist Wasser auf seine Mühlen. Er
verwaltet die Finsternis. Herr ist er
über den Tod

3

"... Es wird ihn Schrecken überfallen wie Wasser,
des Nachts wird ihn das Ungewitter fortnehmen.
Der Ostwind wird ihn wegführen, daß er hinfährt,
und ein Ungestüm wird ihn von seinem Ort treiben.
Er wird solches über ihn führen und wird sein nicht schonen;

He is as mighty as God. The water
in the rivers is his and the black rock
in the mountains. He owns
the meat in the fields and the fish
in the nets. He sets the price
of the crops in the fields. In praise
of his name the forests feed paper
to the mills.

He is more mighty than God. For his sake
the beggars pan the rivers for gold. For his sake
the cold strike fire from the mine-shafts. The rootless
tend his fields. The starving carry grain
to his granaries. To his glory
the homeless build
cities of stone. He is lord
over labourers
and bottle washers.

He is lord of fear. Those who have cried
in protest he has gagged. The angry
he has slain. The Flood
is water for his mills. He rules
the darkness. He is lord
of death.

    3

"... Terrors take hold on him as waters.
A tempest stealeth him away in the night.
The east wind carrieth him away, and he departeth,
and as a storm hurleth him out of this place.
For God shall cast upon him, and not spare;

vor seiner Hand muß er fliehen und wieder fliehen.
Man wird über ihn mit den Händen klatschen
und über ihn zischen, wo er gewesen ist..."

(Hier heißen alle Leute Hiob)

4

Geier hocken auf den Triumphbögen
am Mittag. Der Wind trägt die Gärten
den Wüsten zu. Der Himmel versteinert
über der Stadt. In den Glashäusern
wartet der Schachtelhalm
auf seine Zeit.

(So hörte ich reden)

5

Hier heißen alle Leute Hiob. Die Wälder
kommen als Zeitung ins Haus. Die Berge
erheben sich jenseits der Nacht. Der Himmel
ist ein Mosaik
aus Hinterhöfen.

An den Feuern der Obdachlosen
lege ich mich schlafen. Die Hungernden
teilen mit mir Brot und Tabak. Almosen
empfange ich von den Bettlern. Die Stummen
sprechen mir Mut zu. Die Berge
nenne ich Brüder.

he would fain flee out of his hand.
Men shall clap their hands at him,
and shall hiss him out of his place..."

(Here they call us all Job)

    4

In the middle of the day vultures crouch
on our triumphal arches. The wind carries gardens
into the desert. The sky turns to stone
above the city. In the glass-houses
the snake-grass waits
its moment.

(Or so I have heard)

    5

Here they call us all Job. The forests
land in our houses as newsprint. The mountains
rise far beyond the night. The sky
a mosaic
of back-gardens.

I lie down to sleep
by the fires of the homeless. The starving
share with me their bread and tobacco. I accept
charity from beggars. The dumb
give me words of courage. I call
the mountains my brothers.

Mit den Wäldern tausche ich
den Schatten. Auf dem Wasser der Flüsse
zieht mein Gesicht meerwärts. Der Tag steigt auf
wie ein Wetterleuchten
und vergeht.

6

"Für wen vertut ihr den Tag in Baugruben
und Fabriken? Für welchen Verrat laßt ihr euch
die Taschen füllen am Freitag? Wem gehört
die Villa über dem Fluß? Wen wird die Bombe erschlagen,
die ihr vom Fließband hebt? Für welchen Popanz
haltet ihr die Knochen hin? Seht: Schon flüstern
seine Spitzel über ihn, und seine Söldner
sehen ihn an wie ein Opfer. Dahin ist der Ruhm
und das Glück seines Namens. Die Angst geht an Deck
seiner Schiffe. Wickelt die Fußlappen ab,
die Grabtücher und Fahnen! Nicht länger
soll er die Küsten tränken
mit unserem Blut. Die Spatzen pfeifen
seinen Untergang
von allen Dächern."

7

Heringsschwärme fliegen auf
über den Fischmärkten. Brüllend drängt das Vieh
aus den Schlachthöfen auf die Weiden. Die Berge
fordern ihre Schätze zurück. Die Heimatlosen
erobern das Land. In den Schenken
würfeln die Durstigen
um das Meer.

I exchange my shadow
for the shadow of forests. On the water
of the rivers my face floats seawards. The day
rises like distant lightning
and disappears.

6

"For whose sake do you waste your days
in factories and mines? What will you betray
for a full pocket on Friday? Whose is the villa
across the river? Who will the bomb hit
that you lift from the conveyor-belt? Who is the painted devil
you break your backs to serve? Look: now
his own spies are whispering about him, his mercenaries
treat him as a victim. The fame and the fortune
of his name are gone. Fear walks across the decks
of all his ships. So unwind the footcloths,
the shrouds, the flags! No longer shall he
soak the coasts in our blood. The news
of his downfall travels like fire
across the rooftops."

7

Shoals of herring fly up
over the fish-markets. From the slaughter-houses
cattle surge bellowing on to the pastures. The mountains
claim back their treasures. The rootless
conquer the land. In public houses
the thirsty throw dice to win
the sea.

Große Ereignisse werfen ihr Licht
über die Kontinente. Die Blinden sehen
die Zeichen am Himmel. Die Stummen rufen
die Zukunft aus. Die Ohnmächtigen
übernehmen die Macht.

In den Ebenen senkt der Himmel
seine Wurzeln. Die Flüsse
kehren zurück
zu den Quellen.

Momentous events shed their light
over the continents. The blind
read the signs in the sky. The dumb
proclaim the future. The powerless
seize power.

The sky puts down roots into
the plains. The rivers
flow back
to their source.

AN HÖLTY

Komm, setz dich zu uns! *Noch rauscht*
der schwarze Flügel
des Todes nicht. Wir lassen den Teekessel
für dich singen.

Wir wollen dich bewirten
mit Haselnüssen und Kirschen, ehe der Wind
die Gärten fortträgt. Schlag
die Saiten an!

Pflücke sie weg, o Tod,
die dunkle Blume! Ewigkeiten lieben wir uns,
wie sich Engel lieben. Nimm vorlieb
mit unseren Bräuten!

TO HÖLTY

Come and sit with us. *It is not yet time to*
hear the beat
of death's black wings. We shall fill the kettle
and it will sing for you.

We shall give you
hazelnuts and cherries to eat, before the wind
carries the gardens away. Let us strike up
music from our strings.

Pluck it out, o death,
this dark flower! We shall love for ever
as the angels love. Be content
with our own brides!

Ludwig Hölty (1748-1776) was a member of a group of nature poets known as the Göttinger Hainbund (Grove League of Göttingen). They were influenced by the poet Friedrich Klopstock (1724-1803), who, like von Törne, was born in Quedlinburg. The italicised lines are from Hölty's poems 'Der rechte Gebrauch des Lebens' (The Proper Use of Life) and 'Der Tod' (Death).

POGROM

Für Walter Grab

1

Wie soll ich singen: trocken, ein Knochen
Steckt mir die Zunge im Hals. Scherben
Sind meine Augen. Ein Stein klopft mir
Mein Herz in der Brust. Abhebt die Erde
Sich von meinen Füßen

2

Berge wollt ich versetzen und Kugeln
Aufhalten im Flug mit der Hand. Städte
Wollte ich sehn, voll Sommern und Wintern
Lauschen wollt ich den Stimmen
Der Wälder am Fluß

3

Betten stehen herum wie offene Särge
Stumm wie Steine hocken die Alten
Im Hof. Ein dünnes Blech ist der Himmel
Zerlöchert von Schüssen
Scheppernd im Wind

POGROM

For Walter Grab

1

How can I sing: my tongue is dry,
A bone. It sticks in my throat. My eyes
Are splinters of glass. My heart
A stone that thuds in my chest. The earth
Rises from my feet

2

I dreamt I would move mountains, stop bullets
In mid-air with my hand. I dreamt
I would see cities filled with summers and winters
I dreamt of listening by the river
For the voices of the forest

3

Beds stand about like open coffins
Silent as stones, old people sit
In the yards. The sky is a thin sheet
Of metal, riddled with holes
Clanging in the wind

Walter Grab (1919-2000) was a historian of German democracy. He was born in Vienna and emigrated to Palestine in 1938.

4

Die Wahrheit ist einfach wie Wasser
Und Brot. Ein Netz ist die Nacht
Und der Mensch ein Wild für den Jäger
Meine Haut ist dünn: eine Kugel
Kann mich töten

5

Ohne Abschied werde ich gehn, ohne
Ein Wort, mit zerrissenen Schuhn, den Hut
In der Hand, schutzloses Blut, Asche
Im Wind, wie meine Brüder
Vergessen

4

Truth is simple like water
And bread. The night is a net
And we humans are deer for the hunter
My skin is thin: a bullet
Could kill me

5

I shall go without taking leave, without
A word, with worn-out shoes, holding my hat
In my hand, defenceless flesh, ashes
In the wind, like all my brothers
Forgotten

ERINNERUNG AN EINEN OBERLEHRER

Für den völkischen Staat
ist der gesunde und kräftige
Mensch das höchste Ziel
der Erziehung. Kartoffeln und Kohl
können gleich
in die Markttasche
geschüttet werden. *Unsere Klasse*
macht nächstens
wieder eine Fahrt
ins Blaue

MEMORIAL TO A SCHOOLMASTER

For the good of race and nation
strong and healthy people
must be the primary aim
of education. Without further thought
we can fill
our shopping bags
with cabbages and potatoes.
Soon *our class*
will set off once again
into the unknown

KRÄHENFLÜGEL

Auf der Fensterscheibe dunklem Glas
Seh ich dich fahren, und ich sehe
Schneekahle Äcker und verbranntes Gras
Und überm Bahndamm schwarz die Krähen
Die stumm, wir hören ihre Schreie nicht
Den Winterhimmel kreuzen überm Hügel
Und es streift ein Krähenflügel
Auf der Fensterscheibe dein Gesicht

THE WING OF THE CROW

Across the window pane's darkened glass
I see you glide, and I look out at
Snow-bare fields and burnt-off grass
And above the embankment the black crows fly
In silence – for I cannot hear them cry –
As they cross above the hill in the winter sky
And in the dark glass of the window
Your face is touched by the wing of a crow

AM WEGRAND

Vor langer Zeit
Wir gingen durchs Feld
Meine Mutter hielt
Meine Hand. Am Wegrand
Im Graben kniete ein
Knecht, die Zunge im
Lehmigen Wasser, über
Ihm schwang der Bauer
Die Peitsche: Polak
Steh auf! Weiß wehten
Die Wolken, rot blühte
Am Wegrand
Der Dorn

BY THE WAYSIDE

Once long ago
We walked through these fields
My mother holding
My hand. In a ditch
By the wayside a farm-hand
Crouched, his tongue in
Mud and water, above him
The farmer raising
His whip: On your feet
Polack! Clouds floated
White, the thorn
By the wayside
Flowered red

WEGE DER ASCHE

1

Einst überm Kirchturm erschien mir der Sommer
Ein Engel, zornig mit flammendem Schwert
Der Eichelhäher schrie im Geäst, es brüllte
Das Vieh in den Ställen, im Ofen verbrannte
Das Brot, weiß blühte der Birnbaum, die Sonne
Ein feuriger Wind, brach aus den Wolken

2

Den Rauchzeichen folgend fern überm Land
Zog ich an Flüssen durch flutendes Gras
Durch meine Lungen fuhr brausend der Himmel
Hinter mir sanken die Gärten ins Dunkel
Die Wälder vergingen in Feuer und Rauch
Zu zählen vergaß ich am Wegrand die Krähen

3

Keine Stimme rief mich über den Wassern
Keine Taube senkte sich zu mir herab
Mit Fledermausflügeln beschickte die Nacht
Meine Stirn, mit versteinerter Zunge
Zog ich, allein unterm schweigenden Mond
Die Wege der Asche, begraben im Wind

ON PATHS OF ASHES

1

Above the church tower the summer once seemed
An angry angel, with flaming sword
In the branches a jay screamed, the cows in their stalls
Bellowed out, and the bread in the oven was burned
The pear tree blossomed white, the sun
Broke through, a fiery wind from the clouds.

2

Then I followed the smoke-signals, travelling far
Across country, by rivers, through flooding grass
I felt the rush of the sky through my lungs
Behind me the gardens sank down into dusk
The forests perished in smoke and fire
And I forgot to count the crows on the roadside

3

There was no voice calling me over the waters
There was no dove descending to rest upon me
The night crowned my forehead with wings of bats,
And I moved with a tongue that was turned to stone
Beneath the unspeaking moon alone
On paths of ashes, buried in the wind

4

Was ich auch rede, Worte wie Wolfszähne
Schärfer als Messer, was ich auch rede
Öffne die Lippen: trinken will ich
Deine bittren Wasser, bis du mir zuwächst
Unverlierbar, Fleisch, in das ich mich eingrab
Erde, in der ich wurzle eine kurze Zeit

4

Whatever I say, words like wolves' teeth
More cutting than knives, whatever I say
Open your lips: for I have to drink
From your bitter waters, until you close over me
Flesh, inseparable, I dig myself into
Earth, where briefly I send down my roots

HERBSTFEIER

1

Dunkler rauschen die Wasser am Abend
Und tiefer schweigen die Steine
Im Wind weht des Herbstes Angelschnur
Die Blätter der Bäume erzittern

2

Feiern möcht ich und singen – aber wofür?
In frostige Nacht sank hinunter die schönere Welt
Über Äcker huschen der Hasen hungrige Schatten
Das Halali gefriert im Jagdhorn des Jägers

3

O diese Kälte! An allen Häusern verschlossene Türen
Auf der Blutspur des Lammes geh ich einher unter Wölfen
Zeit ist es heimzukehren in die Stille
Aus einsamer Luft regnet Asche herab

AUTUMN FESTIVAL

1

Darker rush the waters at evening
And deeper grows the silence of stones
In the wind drifts the angling-line of autumn
And the leaves shudder on the trees

2

I would like to dance and sing – but for what?
Now that the world's beauty has sunk into icy night
The hungry shadows of hares flit over the fields
And the mort freezes in the hunter's horn

3

Such cold! The doors are barred on all the houses
I run with the wolves on the track of the lamb's blood
Now it is time to go home to silence
And ashes rain down from the lonely air

SIEGER DER GESCHICHTE

Für Karin und Hans-Richard Nevermann

Was erwartet ihr von mir?
Daß ich von unsern Siegen rede
Daß ich die Hoffnung trage
Auf den Markt der tauben Ohren
Daß ich den Blinden
Ihre Augen öffne
Daß ich die Stummen
Reden lehre?

Ihr wißt wie ich: Das große Babylon
Ging unter, Troja fiel
Und von Mykene blieb nur Stein
Und das Karthagos Mauern schleifte
Das stolze Rom
Zeigt nur noch
Seines Ruhms
Ruinen

Ich frage euch: Was sind
Die Bogenschützen Babylons
Was Hektor und Achill
Was Caesars dröhnende Legionen
Gegen des Pentagons gewaltige Geschwader
Die Horizonte
Kreuzend: die Erde
Im Visier?

HISTORY'S TRUE HEROES

For Karin and Hans-Richard Nevermann

What do you expect me to do?
Tell of our victories
Carry hope to market
And offer it to deaf ears
Open the eyes
Of the blind
Teach the dumb
To speak?

You know as well as I do: mighty Babylon
Was sacked, Troy fell
And Mycene was reduced to rubble
And although it once tore down the walls of Carthage
Now arrogant Rome
Has nothing left
Of its fame
But ruins

Can you tell me: what are
The archers of Babylon
What are Hector and Achilles
What are Caesar's thudding legions
Compared to the Pentagon's vast squadrons
Criss-crossing
The horizons: the earth
In their sights?

Karin and Hans-Richard Nevermann, like von Törne, worked for the *Aktion Sühnezeichen Friedensdienste* (Action Reconciliation-Service for Peace).

Was erwartet ihr von mir?
Daß ich mit einer Feuerpatsche
Den Weltbrand lösche
Daß ich Raketen
Aufhalte mit der Hand
Daß ich mit einem Wort
Die Ledernacken schaffe
Uns vom Hals?

Was wird aus uns?
Wie soll ichs wissen?
Daß wir die Sieger der Geschichte sind
Ist leicht gesagt
Doch weiß ich auch
Wenn wirs nicht werden
Wird diese Erde
Nicht mehr sein

Ich weiß
Daß sich hier nichts bewegt
Wenn wir es nicht bewegen
Es hilft ja nichts:
Wir müssen unsrer Hoffnung
Panzer schmieden
Und Flügel
Unserm Zorn

What do you expect me to do?
Take a fire-beater to the flames
When the whole world is blazing
Put up my hand
To halt the rockets
Speak just a word
To get the leathernecks
Off our backs?

What will become of us?
How should I know?
We are history's true heroes –
That's easily said
But I know for certain
If we fail in this
The earth itself
Will cease to be

I know
That nothing will change
Unless we change it
There's nothing else for it:
We need to forge armour
For our hopes
And wings
For our anger

ELEGIE (1)

Dörfer, windschief im Regen
Wiesen im Weidenlicht
Die sanfte Schönheit
Der Mädchen am Abend
Überm Zaun des Flieders
Duftender Schnee

Land, ausgelöscht
Aus allen Atlanten
Verbrannte Erde, Asche
Von Wurzeln durchbohrt
Worte, geworfen wie Steine
In steigende Wasser

Kürzer werden die Tage
Kälter das Licht
In den Händen nichts
Als meine Trauer
Sammle ich in meinen Augen
Die Scherben des Himmels

ELEGY (1)

Villages, wind-bent in rain
Meadows in willow-light
The gentle beauty
Of girls in the evening
A lilac-tree over the fence
Sweet-smelling snow

This land wiped out
From every atlas
Scorched earth, ashes
Pierced by roots
Words thrown like stones
Into rising waters

The days are growing shorter
And the light colder
In my hands nothing
But grief
In my eyes I gather up
The fragments of the sky

NACHRICHT

Sie haben die Erde
vermessen.
Sie erklären
die Sonne,
durchschauen
den Wind.
Der Regenbogen
ist ihnen untertan. Jetzt

fliegt der Greif. Der Tazzelwurm
schlägt seine Klauen in Beton.

MESSAGE

They have measured
the earth.
They explain
the sun,
interpret
the wind.
The rainbow
is in their power. Now

the Griffin flies. The Tatzelwurm
drives its claws into concrete.

The Tatzelwurm, like the Griffin, is a mythical creature. Whereas the Griffin is part lion and part eagle, the Tatzelwurm, which, according to legend, lives in the Alps, is half cat and half lizard.

ARBEITGEBER

Seine Kinder laufen
barfuß. Seine Frau
geht betteln. Er nagt
am Hungertuch. Weinend
durchforscht er
seine Bilanzen
nach einem kleinen Profit

EMPLOYER

His children go
barefoot. His wife
begs on the streets. He stares
starvation in the face. Looking
through the accounts in tears
he searches
for a tiny profit.

AN ATTILA JÓZSEF

Sohn einer Waschfrau, Schweinehirt:
Häng uns die Wahrheit um
wie einen Wolfspelz! Hör nicht hin, wenn sie sagen:
Geh doch nach drüben.

Bleib bei uns, Bruder, sieh: Unterm erkalteten Himmel
fahren die Monde dahin, hier,
wo wir singen, mit unsern Kindern,
in der Dunkelheit.

Leg dich zu uns, Bruder:
Während wir wachen
gärt der Wein im Dunkel des Kellers, verwandelt der Wind
die Steine in Brot.

Hör zu, Bruder: Der Armen Armut
hat ein Ende! *Auf Lilienfüßen das Blutmeer durchschreitend*
holt uns die Zukunft heim
mit Singsang und Gelächter.

TO ATTILA JÓZSEF

Son of a washerwoman, keeper of pigs,
wrap us in truth
like the skin of a wolf! Do not listen when they say:
Go over there.

Stay with us, brother, look: now the sky has cooled
moons are moving below, here
where we sing, with our children,
in the darkness.

Lie down beside us, brother:
While we keep watch
the wine ferments in the dark of the cellar, and the wind
turns the stones into bread.

Listen, brother: the poor will not be poor
for ever! *Striding through the sea of blood on lotus feet*
the future will fetch us home
with light songs and laughter.

Attila József (1905-1937) was a Marxist Hungarian poet, who also wrote religious poetry.

'Geh doch nach drüben!'(Go over there!) was a phrase often used during the student protests of the late 1960s to those who complained that West Germany was too conservative, or was unwilling to come to terms with its past. 'Over there' was the German Democratic Republic.

Lotus feet were the tiny, mutilated feet of Chinese women who had been subjected to the practice of foot-binding, banned in 1911. A sea of blood is described in the Bible, in Revelation 8:8. The italicised phrase is likely to have come from a news report of the day.

MASURISCHER SOMMER
>   *Für Bohdan Czeszko*

Rauch
Überm Haus. Speck
In der Pfanne. Kuhwarm
Kommt die Milch
Auf den Tisch. Sonne
Im schwarzen Gewölk, das fliegt
Überm Wald mit dem Wind. Adler
Im Licht. Der Kuckuck verkündet
Jahre des Friedens. Hier
Möchte ich bleiben
Behütet
Im Holz

Weitab
Die Straße. Über das Wasser
Wandert der Schatten
Der Wälder. Im Himbeerbusch
Singen die Kinder. Strohdach
Im Erlenlicht. In den Himmel ragt
Des Ziehbrunnes Baum. Nach Heu
Und Holunder duftet
Der Abend. Dem Ufer zu
Treibt unser Kahn. Bleib
Sommer, ruf ich, Hand
Die mich
Hält

SUMMER IN THE MASURIAN LAKES

For Bohdan Czeszko

Smoke
Above the house. *Speck*
Frying in the pan. Milk
On the table
Warm from the cow. Sun
Behind black clouds, flying
Above the forest in the wind. Eagles
In the light. The cuckoo heralding
Whole years of peace. Here
I want to stay
Sheltered
By wood

The road
Far away. Across the water
Forest shadows
Slowly move. Among the raspberry bushes
Children sing. Thatched roof
In alder-light. The tree at
The well outlined by sky. The evening
Filled with scents of hay
And elder. Our boat
Drifts to the bank. Stay, summer,
I shout, hand
That
Holds me.

Bohdan Czeszko (1923-1988) was a Polish writer and screenwriter who had taken part in the Warsaw uprising of 1944.

MITTAGSLICHT

Immer suchen dich meine Augen
Himmel aus blauem Licht Wolken Regen
Und Rauch, Tage aus Honig und Heu
Lerchen im Wind, ins Fenster
Blühen die Rosen, süß reifen
Die Kirschen in meinen Mund

O süßer Duft der Linden im Licht
Fern hinter den Wäldern summen
Die Straßen, über die Ebenen schwarz
Rollen Donner ins Land, unter
Apfelbäumen im wehenden Gras
Gehen pfeifend die Tage dahin

Reden hör ich am Morgen die Stare
Im Kirschbaum vorm Fenster, reden
Hör ich die Steine unter dem Moos
Kühl strömen die Wasser über mich hin
Rot segelt die Sonne, Licht, das ich atme
Die Mündung des Himmels hinauf

Sommer, goldenes Kraut, Dornbusch
Brennend im Wind, nach der Sense
Rufen die Ähren, leer zieh ich
Den Eimer herauf aus dem Brunnen
Rissig ist mein Herz wie die Erde
Die nach Regen schreit

Immer suchen dich meine Augen
Noch einmal will ich die Erde
Ausmessen mit meinem Schritt, siehe
Ich komme zu dir, am Ende des Sommers
Die Taschen voll Nüssen, die Hände
Voll Himmeln aus Licht

MIDDAY LIGHT

My eyes are always drawn to you
Sky full of blue light clouds rain
And smoke, days of honey and hay
Larks in the wind, the roses flowering
In through the window, sweetness
Of cherries ripening into my mouth

In the light the sweet scent of limes
Far beyond the forests the roads
Hum, across the flat land black
Thunder rolls into the countryside, beneath
Apple trees in the waving grass
The days die whistling

In the morning I hear starlings talking
In the cherry tree at the window, I
Hear the stones talking beneath the moss
The waters flow cold over me
The sun sails red, light that I breathe
Up through the estuary of the sky

Summer, leafy gold, thorn-bush
Burning in the wind, the corn calls out
For the scythe, empty I haul
The bucket out of the well
My heart is cracked like the earth
Crying out for rain

My eyes are always drawn to you
Once again I want to pace out
The earth with my steps, look:
I am coming to you, now summer is over
My pockets full of nuts, my hands
Holding skies full of light.

ELEGIE (2)

Wie krieg ich Zärtlichkeit
Und Zorn zusammen in mein Herz
Daß ich mich rege
Kaltes Feuer

Daß deine Hand auf meiner Haut
Mein Fleisch in Wallung bringt
Und meine Knochen
In Bewegung

Bis ich ins Bodenlose falle
Und meine Zunge
Redet stumm
In deinem Mund

Bis ich in deinen Armen liege
Und schlaflos deinem Atem lausche
Der Vögel Stimmen
Die im Stein

Nach den versunknen Ufern rufen
Wo einst mein Messer schnitt
Den Weidenzweig
Und klopfte

Das tönende Holz

ELEGY (2)

How can I find room enough
In my heart for tenderness and rage
That move me to act
Cold fire

That makes your hand upon my skin
Start this surging in my flesh
And this movement
In my bones

Until I fall into endless space
And my tongue
Speaks in your mouth
Without words

Until I lie in your arms
Without sleep, hearing you breathe
And the voices of birds
Calling from rocks

For those buried banks
Where once my knife cut
Willow switches
And I tapped

The sounding wood

AM SCHREIBTISCH

Mein Schädel
Ein Dachboden
Ich krame herum
In Worten
Abgetragen
Und längst
Aus der Mode
Tage und Träume
Alte Fotos
Vergilbt
Und vergessen
Die frühen Küsse
Strohblumen
Hinter Spinnengeweb
Nächte
Aus Müdigkeit
Und Liebe
Blätter
Getrocknet
Zwischen den Seiten
Eines alten
Kalenders
Leere Flaschen
Die Räusche
Von gestern

Am Schreibtisch
Sitzt einer
Der trägt
Meinen Namen
Und schreibt:
Ich sehe dich an
Und sehe
Den Himmel

AT THIS DESK

My skull
An attic
I rummage
Through words
Worn thin
And long
Out of fashion
Days and dreams
Old photographs
Faded and
Now forgotten
First kisses
Dried flowers
Covered in webs
Nights
Of sleeplessness
And love
Leaves
Pressed
Between the pages
Of an old
Calendar
Empty bottles
Yesterday's
Drunken ecstasy

At this desk
There sits a man
Who bears
My name
He writes:
I look at you
And see
The sky

Gespiegelt
In deinen Augen
Manchmal
Berühren sich
Unsere
Hände

Mirrored
In your eyes
Now and again
Our hands
Make contact

DIESSEITS

Hier laß ichs mir wohlsein
Genieß ich mein Leben
Zwischen Wannsee und Tegel
Unterm Geheul der Clipper von PAN
Mitten im Dreck der Motore
Bin ich zuhaus
Wohn ich zur Miete
Richt ich mich ein
Schlage ich Wurzeln
Auf dem freien Wohnungsmarkt
Zwischen Supermärkten Massagesalons
Dem Wetterbericht der Morgenandacht
Nazirichtern Rockern GIs
Siemens dem Fließband der Deutschen Bank
Der Freiheitsglocke der Marktwirtschaft
Der Mode dem Müll den steigenden Preisen
Dem anonymen Anrufer um Mitternacht
Dem Gift das ins Grundwasser sickert
Hier tast ich nach Licht
Such ich den Ausgang

OVER HERE

Things are very pleasant here
And I enjoy my life
Here between Tegel and the Wannsee
Beneath the droning PAN-AM airliners
Among the filth of car-engines
I feel at home
In a rented flat
I have set up house
Put down roots
In the private rented sector
Among supermarkets massage-parlours
Weather forecast morning service
Nazi judges rockers GIs
Siemens the Deutsche Bank production line
Free market economy Liberty Bell
Fashions waste rising prices
The anonymous caller at midnight
Toxins seeping into our ground-water
I am groping towards the light here
Looking for the way out

IM FAHRTWIND

Vom Fließband rollen
Die verschwitzten Tage, aus
Plastiktüten steigt
Des Feierabends kurzer
Atem, erloschen sind
Die Neonsonnen, leer
Die Straßen, morgen
Ist Sonntag, und die Leute
Glauben an ein Leben
Nach dem Tod

Stülp dir den Sturzhelm
Übern Schädel, zeig
Der Welt dein Rücklicht
Die Sterne spiegeln sich
Auf deinem Rücken im
Schwarzen Lack der Lederjacke
Im Fahrtwind glaubst du
Daß du lebst

IN THE RUSH OF AIR

Days damp with labour
Roll off the production-line, from
Plastic bags rises
The brief breath of
After-work hours, neon
Suns switched off, streets
Empty, tomorrow
Is Sunday, and we'll
All believe in life
After death

Shove your crash-helmet
On your skull, turn
Your rear-light to the world
The stars are mirrored
On your back in the
Black gleam of your leather jacket
In the rush of air you believe
You're alive

NACHMITTAGSBESUCH

Auf dem Tisch Blumen, die Teekanne
Flaschen, Tassen und Gläser. Silvi
Trägt einen Teller mit Waffeln
Herein. Johannes sieht
In sein Glas und spinnt
Sein Seemannsgarn. Natascha
Malt uns das Bild
Auf dem wir wegfliegen
Können. Wenn wir
Lange genug hinsehn
Wachsen uns
Flügel

AN AFTERNOON VISIT

There are flowers on the table, a teapot
Bottles, cups and glasses. Silvi
Bringing a plate of waffles
In. Johannes staring
Into his glass and spinning
His sailor's yarn. Natasha
Paints a picture for us to fly away
On. If we look at it
For long enough
We shall grow
Wings

VATERLANDSLOS

Denn nichts als Verzweiflung kann uns retten
CHRISTIAN DIETRICH GRABBE

Vater
Lands
Los, in
Meiner
Mutter
Sprache
Zuhaus
Um mich
Die Wand
Aus Büchern
Eine Mauer
Gegen
Den Tod
Verzweiflung
Rettet uns
Nicht

FREE OF MY FATHERLAND

For only despair can save us
　　　　　Christian Dietrich Grabbe

Free
Of my Father
Land,
At home
In my
Mother
Tongue
Around me
The wall
Of books
A barrier
Against
Death
Despair
Cannot
Save us

Christian Dietrich Grabbe (1801-1836) was a German dramatist, a forerunner of Realism in the German theatre.

EPIGRAMM

Fleißig sind wir und ordentlich
Deshalb lieben die anderen Völker
Uns Deutsche: Überall
Räumen wir auf

EPIGRAM

We Germans: hard-working, respectable
That's why other nations
Love us; always so good
At clearing up

FRÜHLINGSGEDICHT

Frisch gewaschen
Flattert der Himmel
Hinterm Zaun
Aus Antennen
Der Kastanienbaum
Vor meinem Fenster
Entfaltet Blätter
Aus Wurzeln
Unterm Asphalt
Jenseits der Straße
Sehe ich in der Sonne
Die weiße Brust
Einer Katze

SPRING SONG

Newly washed
The sky flaps
Behind
The fence of aerials
Its roots
Beneath the asphalt
The chestnut tree
By my window
Unfolds new leaves
Across the street
The sun catches
The white of
A cat's breast

FLUGBLATT

Du auf der Lichtung,
wo die Fledermaus schwirrt,
unterwandert von Grillen:
Blas dein Strohfeuer an. Rupf
den Spatzen in deiner Hand.
Begieß ihn mit Pech. Schmor ihn
im rostigen Helm. Sei fröhlich,
und laß es dir schmecken!

FLYER

You there in the clearing
with the whirring bats
infiltrated by grasshoppers:
blow on your brief blaze. Pluck
the sparrow you hold in your hand.
Pour tar over it. Roast it
in your rusty helmet. Be cheerful
and enjoy your meal.

SELBSTGESPRÄCH

Warum sollen deine Verse
haltbarer sein
als die Blätter des Baums
vor dem Fenster?

Von den Lebendigen sprich
nicht wie von den Toten. Rede vom Feuer,
das hinfährt, donnernd,
über die Städte.

Sprich von Vergänglichem. Aber
sprich gegen den Tod.

SOLILOQUY

Why should your poems
live longer
than the leaves on a tree
by the window?

Do not speak of the living
as you speak of the dead. Talk of the fire,
the thunder which rushes
above the cities.

Speak of things which die. But
speak out against death.

RÜCKZUG

Fragt nicht
Nach mir

Die Richtung
Des Windes
Kann ich
Nicht ändern

Ohne Hut
Steh ich
Im Regen

So weit
Ist es
Gekommen

Freunde

WITHDRAWAL

Do not ask
About me

I cannot
Change
The direction
Of the wind

I am standing
In the rain
With no hat

This is
How far
Things have gone

Friends

NOTSTAND

Dieben
Vertraute ich
Mein Haus an

Lügnern
Gab ich
Meine Stimme

Mörder
Bewachen
Meinen Schlaf

STATE OF EMERGENCY

To thieves
I have entrusted
My house

To liars
I have lent
My voice

Murderers
Watch over
My sleep

ANRUFUNG MEINES ENGELS

Was ist geschehn? Der Wind schlug um
Der Himmel klirrt von früher Kälte
In Leitartikeln kriecht der Krieg. Schon
Sind die Marschbefehle unterschrieben
Die Hinterhöfe sind umstellt

Ich hör ein Rauschen in der Luft
Was wolln wir tun mit all den Waffen
Die sie auf unser Dach, auf unsre Schultern
Unsre Haut gehäuft? Was braucht
Die Liebe? Nichts. Nur dich und mich

In welche Dunkelheit läßt du dich fallen?
Ich habe Angst um dich und deinen Atem
Um deine Schädelknochen unter dünner Haut
Heb deinen Kopf und laß uns reden
Eh uns ein Stiefel auf die Kehlen tritt

Daß ich nicht schlafen kann, muß nichts
Bedeuten. Und wärs die Stunde, da Raketen
Von fernen Rampen steigen: eh unsre Hände
In die Kälte greifen, laß mich noch einmal
Deinen Atem spüren auf der Haut

I CALL UPON MY ANGEL

What has happened? The wind has changed
The leaves rattle with sudden winter
War lurks in the editorials. Now
The marching orders are signed,
And the back-gardens surrounded

I hear a roaring in the air
What do we want with all these weapons
They have piled on our roofs, on our shoulders
On our skin? What does
Love need? Nothing. Just you and me

What is that darkness you let yourself fall into?
I'm afraid for you, for your breath
The bones of your skull beneath fragile skin
Lift up your head so we can talk
Before someone's boot comes down on your throat

If I can't sleep, it doesn't mean much.
And even if, this hour, rockets are fired
From distant ramps: before our hands
Reach into cold, let me again
Feel your breath upon my skin

BEIM LESEN DER ZEITUNG

Ich lese in der Zeitung, daß die Mörder
Von Mord und Totschlag nichts gewußt.
(Meine Schwester nähte damals
ihren Puppen gelbe Flicken auf die Brust.)

WHILE READING THE PAPER

Butchers 'didn't know' of slaughter
– so at least the papers say.
(And I watched my sister with her dolls
Sewing yellow patches on in play.)

STUNDE DER WÖLFE

Stunde
Der Wölfe
Die Lieder der Mädchen
Verstummten
Im Dorf

Den Flug
Der Taube kreuzte
Der Habicht, fort trugen
Die Schwalben
Das Licht

Stimmen
Wie Rufe, fern
Aus dem Dunkel, Schnee
Wehte der Wind
Auf den Weg

HOUR OF THE WOLVES

Hour
Of the wolves, and
The songs of the girls in
The village
Fell still

The flight
Of the dove cut
Across by the hawk, the
Swallows transported
The light

Voices
Like calls, from away
In the darkness, wind
Drove snow over
The path

GEDANKEN IM MAI

Ich rede von mir: Volker von Törne, geboren
Im vierunddreißigsten Jahr des zwanzigsten Jahrhunderts
Als meine Genossen schon kämpften gegen die Mörder
Die mich aufzogen als ihresgleichen
Nach ihrem Bilde:
                Und ich trank die Milch
Die dem Hungernden fehlte. Und ich trug das Kleid
Meinem Bruder geraubt. Und ich las die Bücher
Die den Raub billigten. Und ich hörte die Reden
Die aufriefen zum Mord:
                      Und ich nannte den Schlachthof
Mein Vaterland, als schon die Völker aufstanden
Gegen mein Volk. Und ich betete für den Endsieg
Der Mörder, als schon die Städte
Aufgingen in Rauch:
                Und schuldig war ich
Am Tod jedes Menschen, ahnungslos atmend
Unter den Galgenästen
Süßduftender Linden

THOUGHTS IN MAY

I speak of myself: Volker von Törne, born
In the thirty-fourth year of the twentieth century
While my comrades were fighting the murderers
Who brought me up as their own
In their image:
          And I drank the milk
Denied to the starving. And I wore the clothes
Stolen from my brother. And I read the books
Justifying the theft. And I listened to speeches
Inciting to murder:
          And I called that slaughter-house
My fatherland, while the nations took up arms
Against my nation. And I prayed for the murderers,
For their final victory, while the cities
Went up in flames:
          And mine was the guilt
For the loss of every life, breathing in innocence
Under the gallows-branches
Of the sweet-smelling limes

BILDER

Daß ich die Augen schließe
Die Sicherung rausdreh
Den Bildschirm zertrümmre
Was nützt es: Bilder
Regnen ins Zimmer, erweichen
Die Wände, den Schädelknochen
Mein Hirn, vor Augen die Hand
Seh ich nicht mehr, ich tappe
Im Bunten

IMAGES

If I close my eyes
Pull out the fuse
Smash the screen
Where does it get me: images
Rain into my room, softening
The walls, the bone of my skull
My brain; now I am completely
In the dark, feeling my way
Through coloured light

AN AHASVER

Auf den Gräbern der Welt
sitzt du und singst
deine Psalmen,
die Asche der Toten
zu wecken
und ihnen Schuhe zu nähen
für den Weg zurück – :

Nimm die Binde ab,
zeig uns
deine Stirn!

TO AHASUERUS

On the graves of the world
you sit and sing
your psalms,
to awaken
the ashes of the dead
stitching them shoes
for their journey back – :

Take off your blindfold,
look life
in the face.

In Christian legend, Ahasuerus was a shoemaker who taunted Jesus on the way to the Crucifixion and in return was condemned to wander the earth until Jesus returned. He became known as the Wandering Jew, appearing in places as far apart as Newcastle and Prague in the seventeenth and eighteenth centuries.

AN HÖLDERLIN

Durch den Blutregen kommst du
mit Haut und Haaren
und einem Mund voller Oden
durch Galgenwälder
dem Windwasser folgend
auf den Spuren
eines flüchtigen Traums – :

Mach Kleinholz
aus deinem Drachenschiff, o Bellarmin!

Mit Fundevogels Federn
und den Scherben des Glasbergs
beladen mit Füllhörnern
und Wünschelruten
gehst du und klopfst
den Himmel ab
nach dem verschütteten Meer.

TO HÖLDERLIN

You've come through a rain of blood
with body and soul intact
your mouth filled with odes
through forests of gallows
following wind-water
on the track of
a vanishing dream – :

Make matchwood
of your dragon-ship, o Bellarmin!

Laden with the feathers of the Fundevogel
with fragments of the glass mountain
horns of plenty
and divining rods
you go on your way
tapping the heavens
in search of the buried sea.

Bellarmin appears in the novel *Hyperion* by German poet Friedrich Hölderlin (1770-1843), as the recipient of Hyperion's letters. The italicised sentence is not a quotation from Hölderlin.
    According to Grimms' Fairy Tales, Fundevogel was a foundling child who had been snatched from his mother by a large bird.

NOTSTANDSÜBUNG

Mit Wasserwerfern
bekämpfen sie
die Sintflut.

Mit Gummiknüppeln
öffnen sie uns
die Augen.

Im Licht ihrer Lügen
erkennen wir
die Wahrheit.

EMERGENCY DRILL

With water-cannon
they fight
the Flood.

With rubber truncheons
they open
our eyes.

In the light of their lies
we see
the truth.

EISZEIT

Ja
Es ist finster
Geworden
Leitartikel
Nageln sie
Wie Bretter
Vor deinen Kopf
Wie einen Knebel
Stoßen sie dir
Neue Gesetze
In den Hals

Ja
Zu einem Rädchen
Machen sie dich
In ihrer
Knochenmühle
Lebendig
Begraben sie dich
Unterm Müll
Ihrer Märkte

Ja
Es ist kälter
Geworden
Im Winde
Klirren
Die Fahnen

ICE AGE

Yes
It has grown
Dark
They nail up
Leading articles
Like boards
In front of your face
Like a gag
They push
New laws
Down your throat

Yes
They make you
A cog
In their
Bonemeal grinder
They bury you
Alive
Beneath the waste
In their markets

Yes
It has grown
Colder
In the wind
The clinking
Of weathervanes

The italicised lines are from Friedrich Hölderlin's poem 'Hälfte des Lebens' (Half of Life).

ERINNERUNG AN CARL SANDBURG

There are men who can't be bought

Stürme werden dies Land
zerschlagen. Sammle die Sterne,
wenn du es magst. Alles muß einfach sein
für einen Henker.

Was tut Gott, wenn er einsam ist?
Das sind so Fragen.

REMEMBERING CARL SANDBURG

There are men who can't be bought

Storms will batter and break this land.
Pick up the stars,
if you feel so inclined. Everything must be simple
for a hangman.

What does God do, when he's lonely?
these are the things people ask.

Carl Sandburg (1878-1967) was an American poet, the son of a Swedish immigrant. The epigraph is from his 1936 poem 'The People, Yes'.

AUF DEM BODEN DES GRUNDGESETZES (1976)

Mit beiden Füßen fest
Auf dem Boden des Grundgesetzes
Erkläre ich: So wie es ist
Wird es bleiben. Bis ans Ende
Aller Tage hat unsere freiheitlich
Demokratische Grundordnung
Bestand. Nur Kommunisten
Wagen zu behaupten, unsere Welt
Sei nicht die beste Welt
Aller Welten. Nur Ketzer
Zweifeln daran, daß
Die Sonne sich dreht
Um die Erde

THE CONSTITUTION (1976)

Both feet firmly planted
In the soil of our German Constitution
I make my statement: as it is now,
So it will always be. Until the end
Of time our basic principles
Of freedom and democracy
Shall hold. Only the Communists
Dare assert that this world
Is not the best
Of all possible worlds. And only heretics
Question whether
The sun really revolves
Around the earth.

KRIEGSSPIEL

Auf der Straße
Spielen die Kinder
Krieg, bald
Wenn sie größer sind
Spielt der Krieg
Mit ihnen

WAR GAME

The children
In the street play
A game of war; soon
They'll be bigger
And war will play games
With them

REGIERUNGSERKLÄRUNG

Die Regierung der USA bedauert,
daß sie den Kampf gegen die Armut
hat einstellen müssen,
um den Krieg
gegen die Armen
fortführen zu können.

Besorgt suchen die Augen
der Bauern, die den Boden
für den Reis bereiten,
den Himmel ab.

A STATEMENT BY THE GOVERNMENT

The government of the USA regrets
it must put on hold
the war on poverty
in order to facilitate
the war
against the poor.

Full of fear the eyes
of farmers preparing
the ground for rice
search the skies.

PASTORALE

1

O Morgen, birkengrün und duftend
Nach frischem Brot
Aprilregenkühl
Deine Küsse

2

Staubfahnen entfaltet der Sommer
Über den Wegen, es welken
Im Kornfeld die Wurzeln
Des Windes

3

Am Wegrand ein Kind, im Haar
Kornblumen und Mohn, schärfer
Werden die Schatten
Im Licht

4

Durch die Wälder singen
Die Sägen, kopflos
Flattern Hühner
Im Hof

PASTORAL

1

Birch-green morning, with the
Scent of fresh bread,
Cool as April rain
Your kisses

2

The summer unrolls waves of dust
Across the paths, in the cornfield
The roots of the wind
Wither

3

By the path a child, in her hair
Cornflowers and poppies, the light
Makes the shadows
Sharpen

4

Through the forests saws
Sing, in the farmyard
Hens flutter
Headless

5

Nichts weiß ich über den Anfang
Nichts weiß ich über das Ende
Ich bewege, was mich
Bewegt

5

I know nothing of the beginning
I know nothing of the end
What I move is what
Moves me

TRINKSPRUCH

Adolf Hitler lebte fade
Denn er trank nur Limonade
Später aber soff er dann
Blut als wie der Tamerlan
Hätt er Bier und Schnaps gesoffen
Wärs vielleicht nicht eingetroffen

DRINKING SONG

Hitler's life was deadly dull
Cos he drank no alcohol
Later on this boring man
Drank more blood than Genghis Khan
If he'd had more taste for ale
We'd not have had this sorry tale

LIEBESGEDICHT

Schwarz
Eine Katze
Auf windweichen Pfoten
Kommt über die Dächer
Die Nacht

Schwer
Von Sternen
Hängen die Zweige
Des Himmels über
Dem Haus

Verhäng
Die Fenster
Zünd an ein Licht
Wie schön du bist, sag ich
Wie schön

LOVE POEM

Black
A cat
On wind-soft paws
The night comes over
The roofs

Heavy
With stars
The branches of the sky
Hang up above
The house

Close
The curtains
Put on a light
How beautiful you are, I say
How beautiful

ZU BEGINN DER ACHTZIGERJAHRE. NACH CATULL

Was, Törne, hält vom Tode dich noch ab?
Der alte Schrecken geht einher in neuen Waffen
Die Angst hat Flügel und der Zorn ist kalt
Was, Törne, hält vom Tode dich noch ab?

AT THE START OF THE EIGHTIES: AFTER CATULLUS

And what, von Törne, keeps you now from death?
The older terrors speak with modern guns
Fear has wings and anger has grown cold
And what, von Törne, keeps you now from death?

The poem is based on 'Carmen 52' (Poem 52) by the Latin poet
Catullus (84-54 BC).

BIOGRAPHICAL NOTES

Volker von Törne, was born on 14 March 1934 in Quedlinburg, a town just north of the Harz Mountains, Germany. He moved to Berlin in 1962 and in 1963 became a Director of Aktion Sühnezeichen Friedensdienste (Action Reconciliation-Service for Peace), a role in which he developed the idea of an International Youth Meeting Centre in Oświęcim / Auschwitz, an idea that was finally realised some years after his death. During his many years at the head of the ARSP, he became emotionally attached to numerous Auschwitz survivors in many European countries. His personal process of coming to terms with his family history as the son of an SS unit commander made him into one of the most important German dialogue partners in Europe for the survivors. He died on 30 December 1980. His life and work are still commemorated throughout Europe.

Jean Boase-Beier is a translator of poetry from and into German, and is Emeritus Professor of Literature and Translation at the University of East Anglia. She has written many academic works on translation, poetry and style: recent publications include *Stylistic Approaches to Translation* (2006, St Jerome Publishing), *A Critical Introduction to Translation Studies* (2011, Bloomsbury) and *Translating the Poetry of the Holocaust* (2015, Bloomsbury). Jean Boase-Beier's poetry translations include Ernst Meister *Between Nothing and Nothing* (2003) and Rose Ausländer *While I Am Drawing Breath* (2013) both from Arc Publications. She is Arc Publications' Translations Editor, and the series editor of the 'Visible Poets' and 'Arc Classics' series.

ANTHONY VIVIS, who died in October 2013, was a playwright and translator who played a leading role in introducing postwar German drama to the English-speaking world. A former dramaturg with the Royal Shakespeare Company and BBC Drama editor, he was best known for his translation of plays by dramatists such as Manfred Karge, Rainer Werner Fassbinder, Gerlind Reinshagen and Franz Xaver Kroetz. He collaborated on a number of translated poetry collections including *The Brontës' Hats* (1991, Reality Street Editions) by Sarah Kirsch, which he translated together with Wendy Mulford.

DAVID WHEATLEY (born 1970) is an Irish poet and critic. He was born in Dublin and studied at Trinity College, Dublin, where he edited *Icarus*. He is the author of five volumes of poetry, four from Gallery Press – *Thirst* (1997), *Misery Hill* (2000), *Mocker* (2006) and *A Nest of Waves* (2010) – and the most recent, *The President of Planet Earth* (2017), from Carcanet. He has also published several chapbooks. He has edited the work of James Clarence Mangan, and features in the Bloodaxe anthology *The New Irish Poets* (Bloodaxe, 2005), and the *Wake Forest Irish Poetry Series Vol. 1* (Wake Forest UP, 2005). He teaches at the University of Aberdeen, having previously taught at Hull. He was shortlisted for the Poetry Now Award, in 2007, and was awarded The Vincent Buckley Poetry Prize, in 2008.